This Book Belongs To :

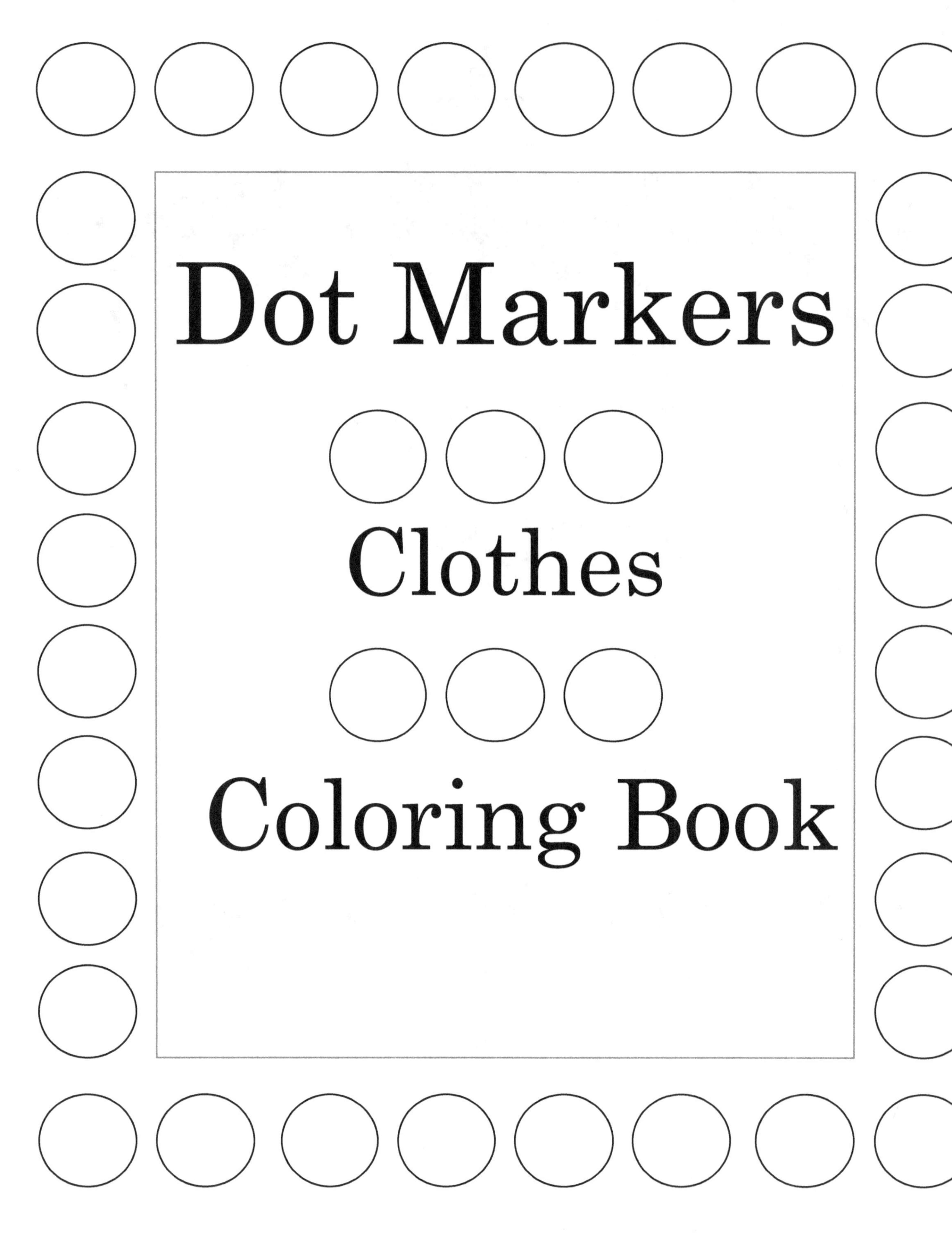

Dot Markers
Clothes
Coloring Book

T-shirt

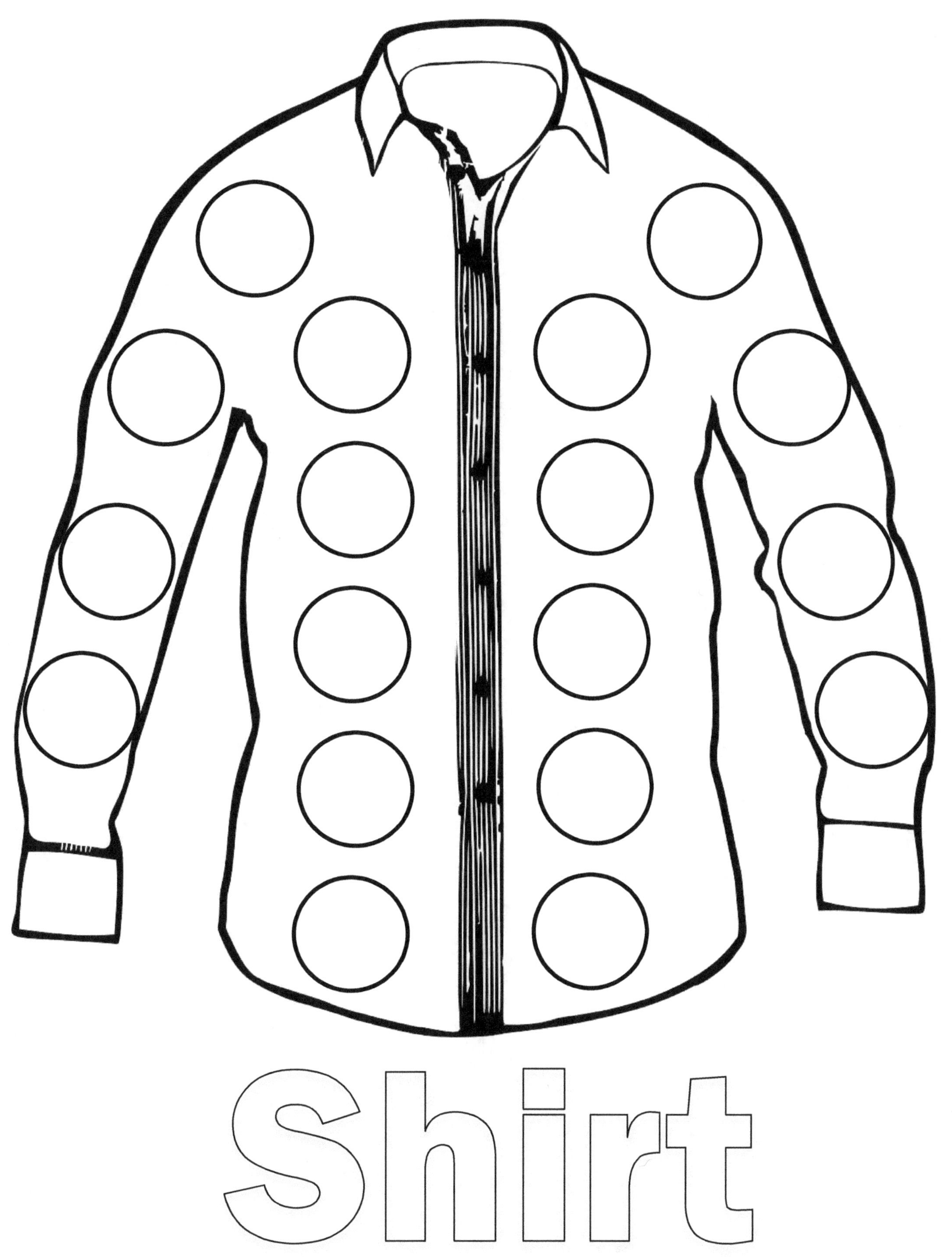

Shirt

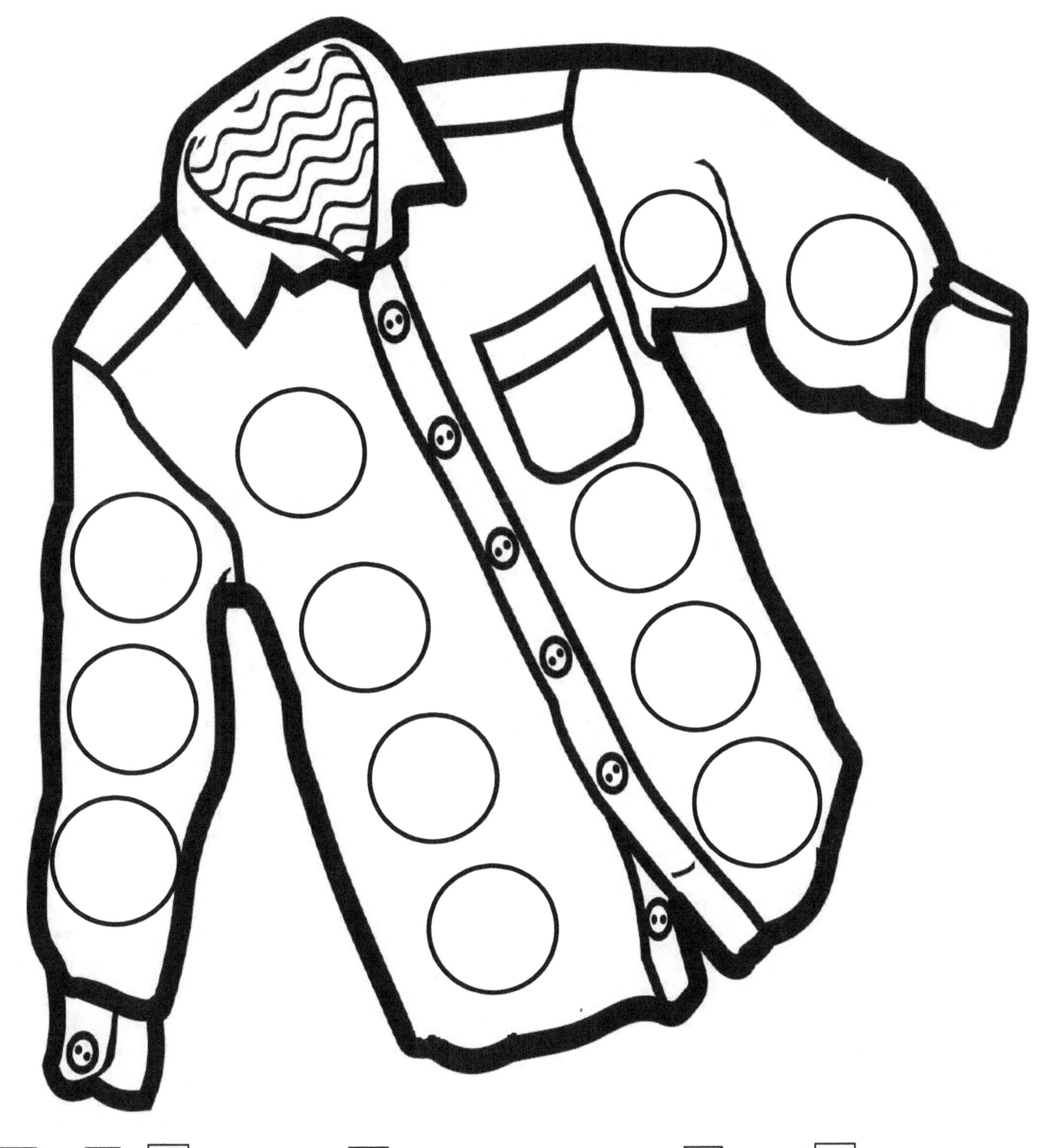

Nightshirt

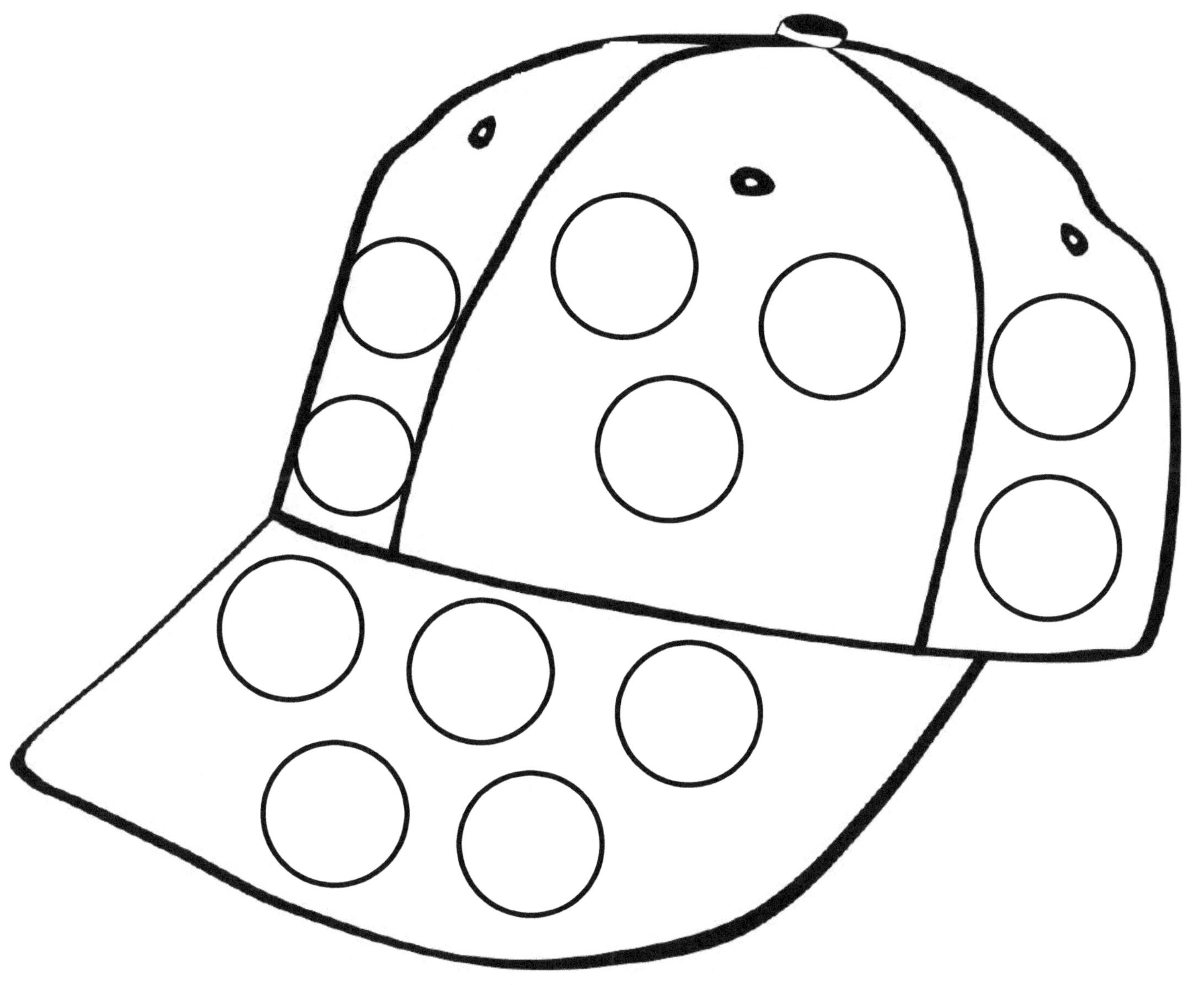

Hat

Classic hat

Graduation hat

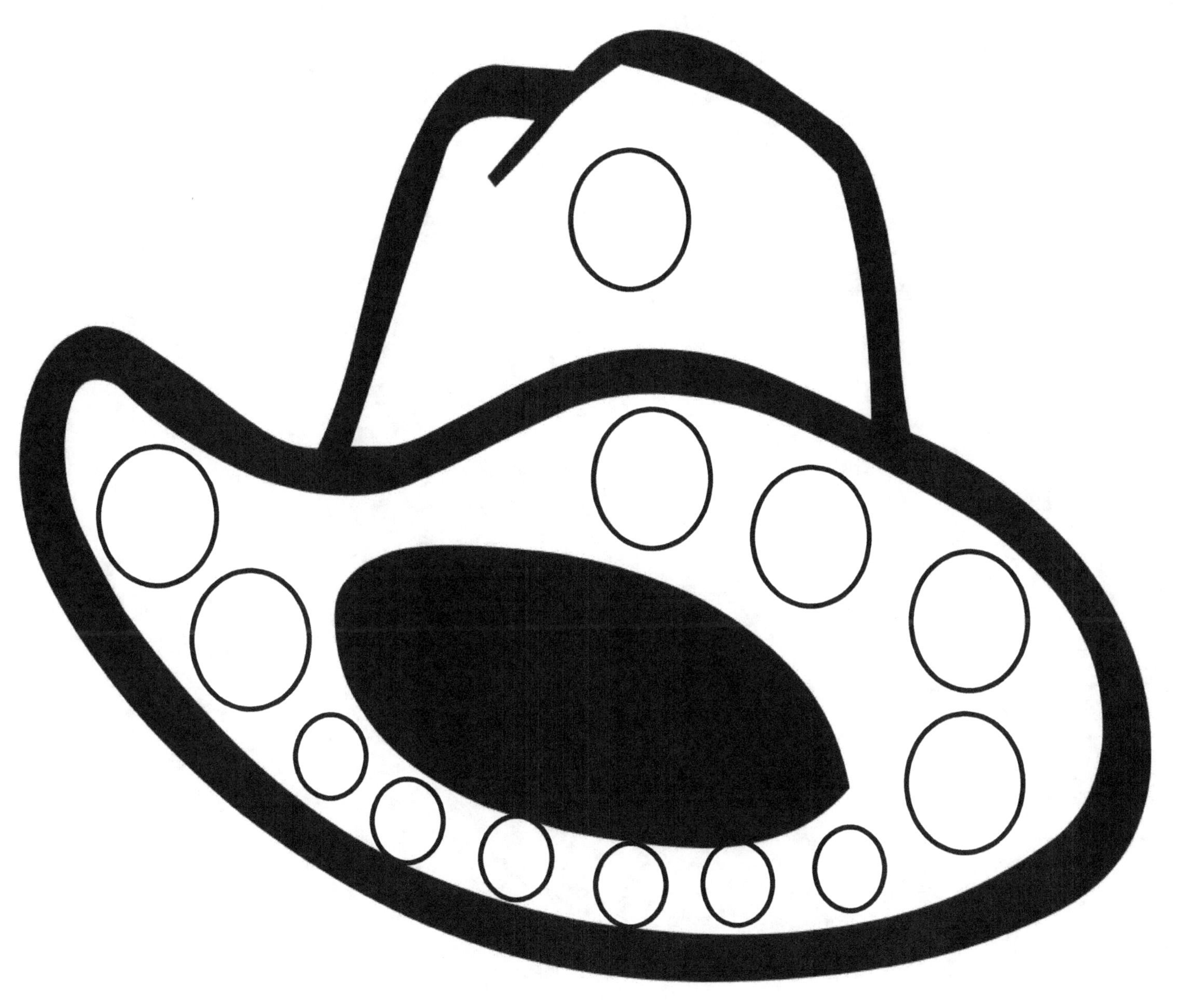

Cowboy
hat

Women's hat

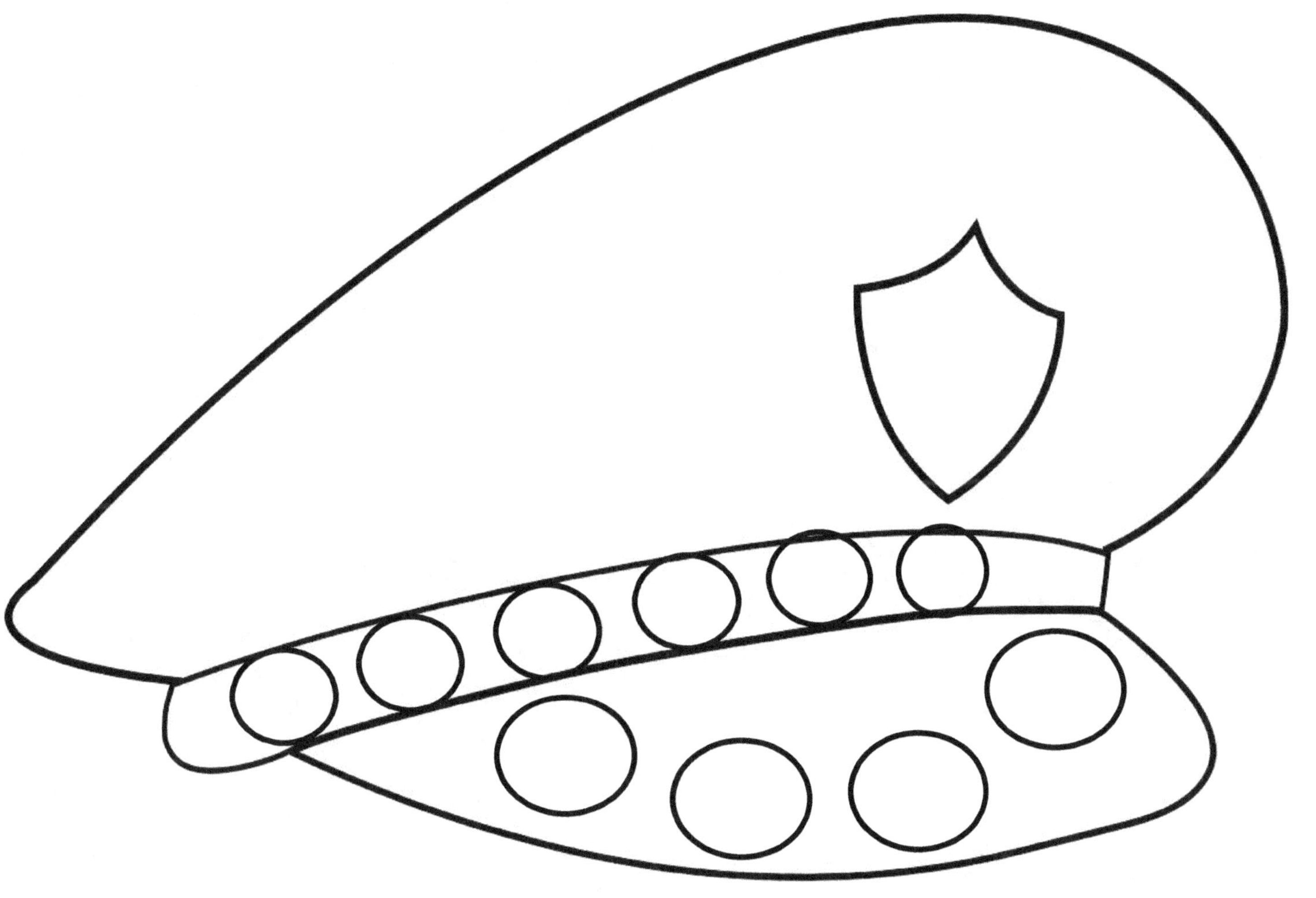

Police hat

Magician
hat

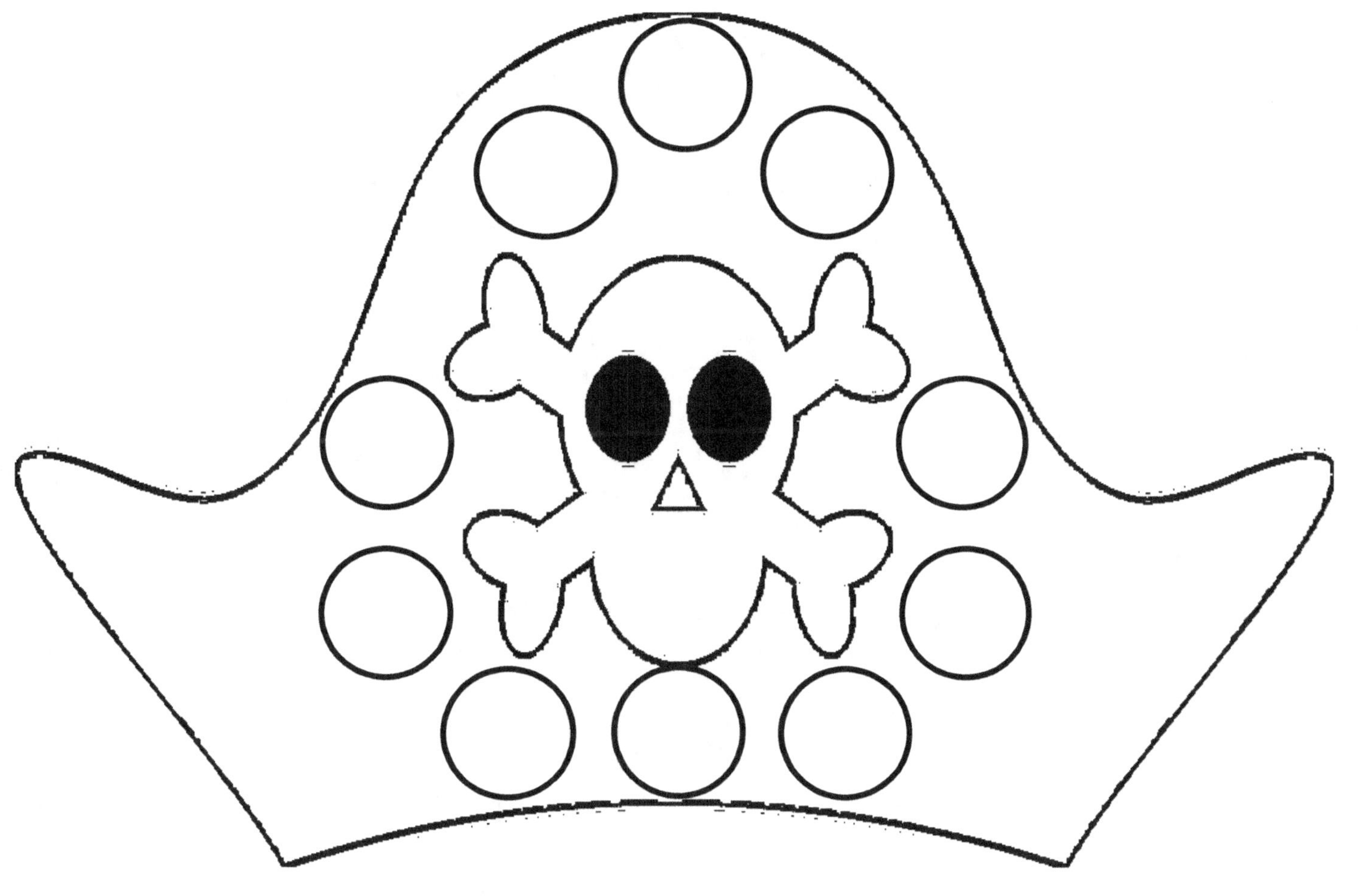

Pirate hat

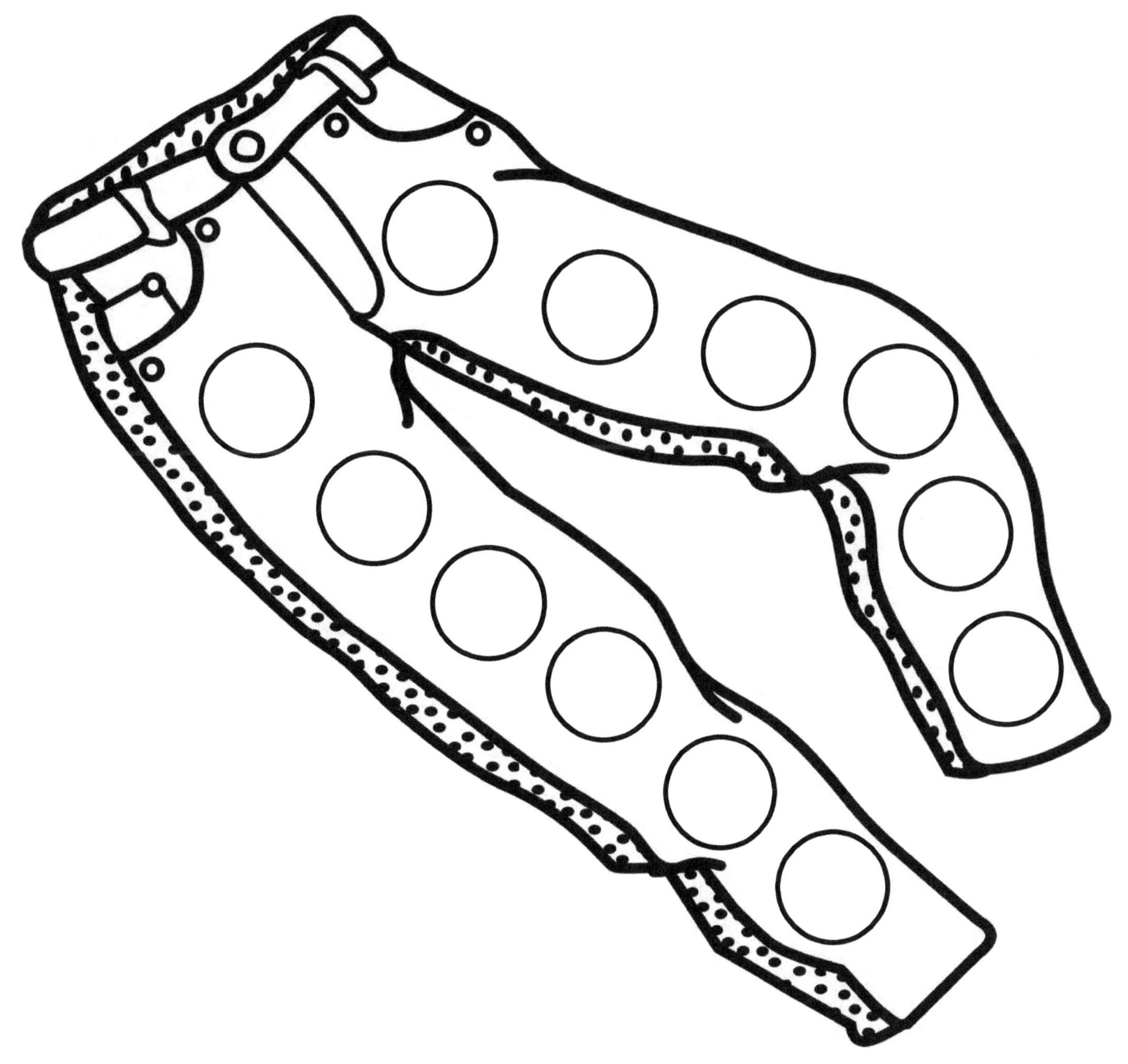

Trousers

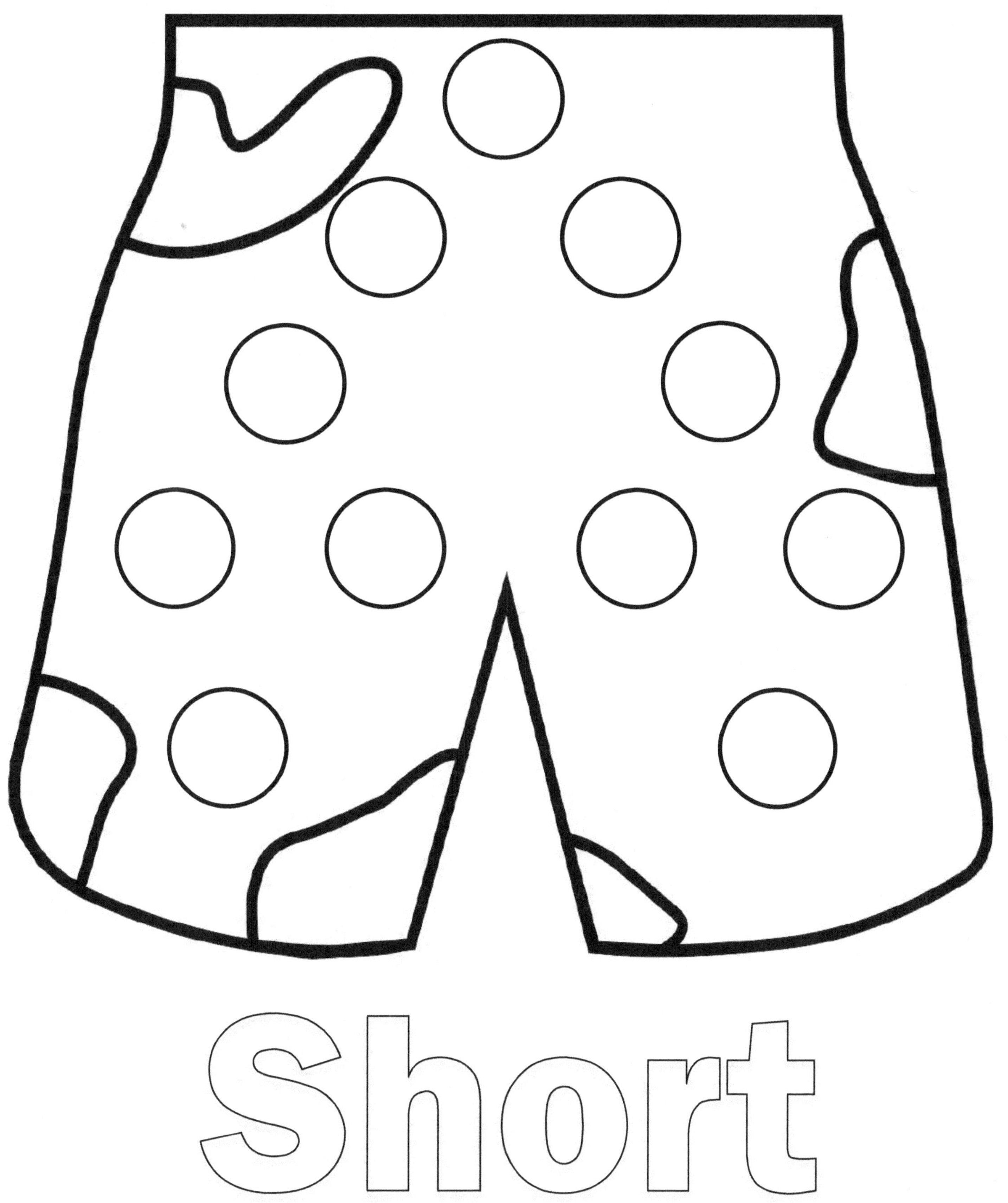
Short

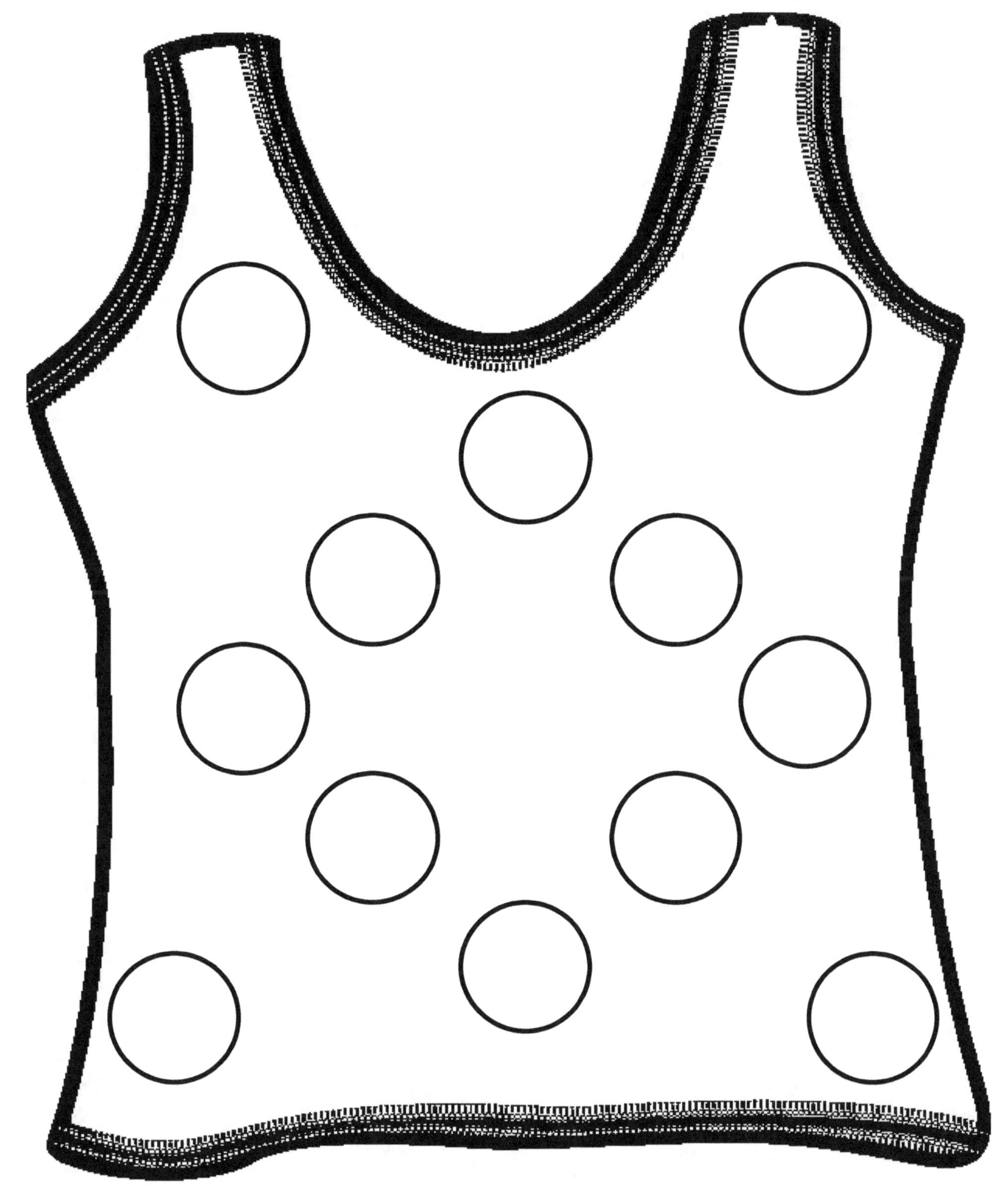
Undershirt

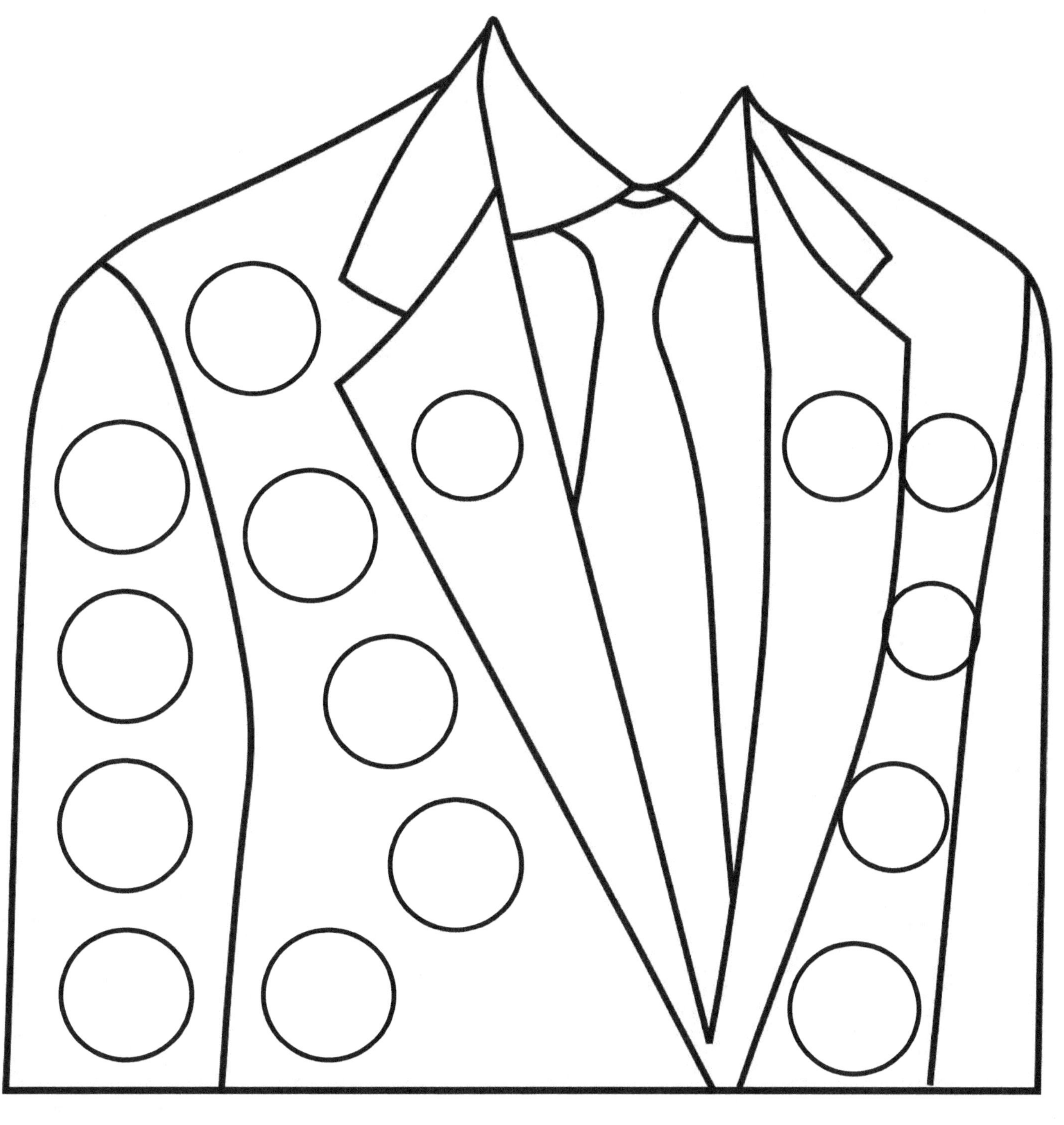

Costume

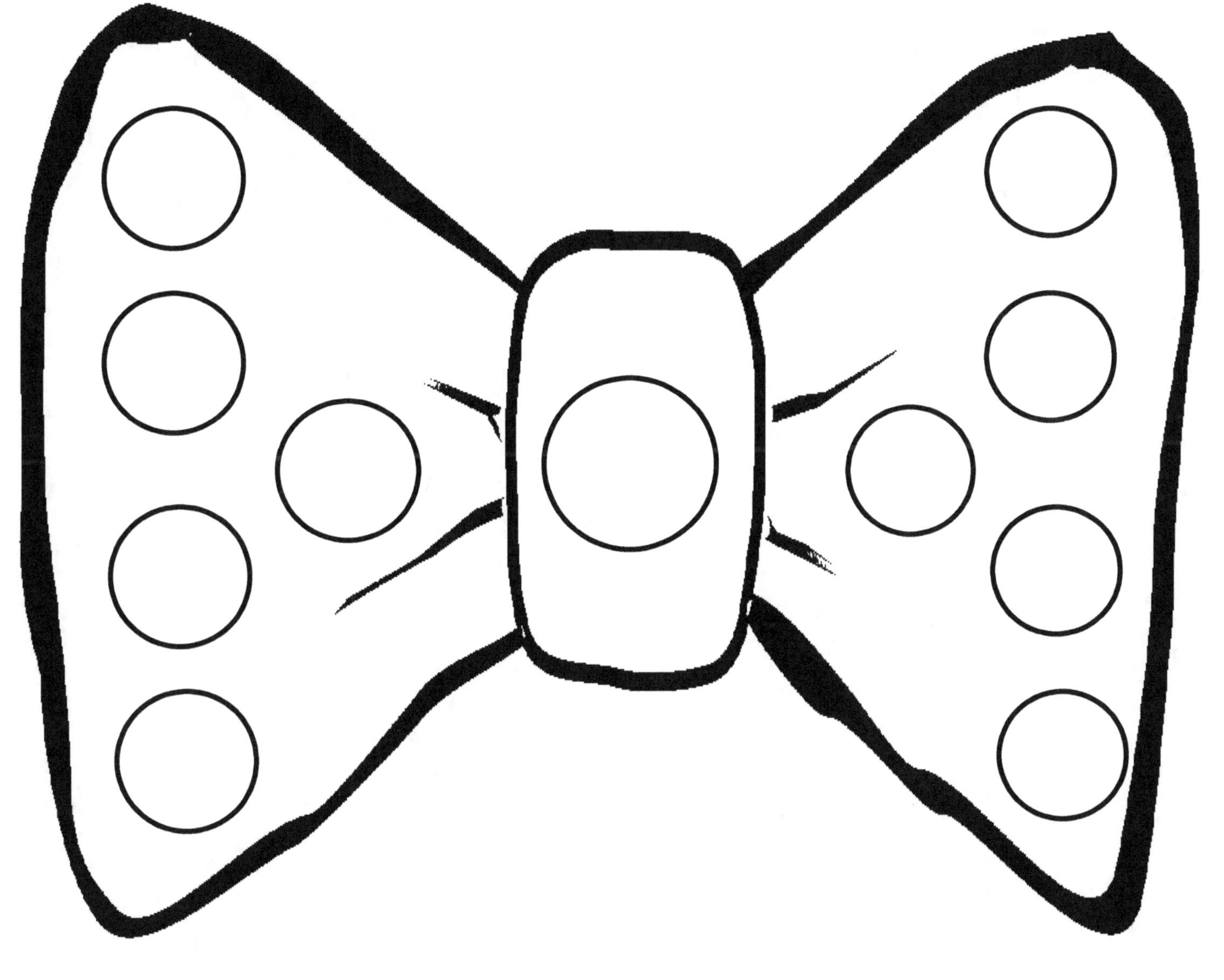

Bow tie

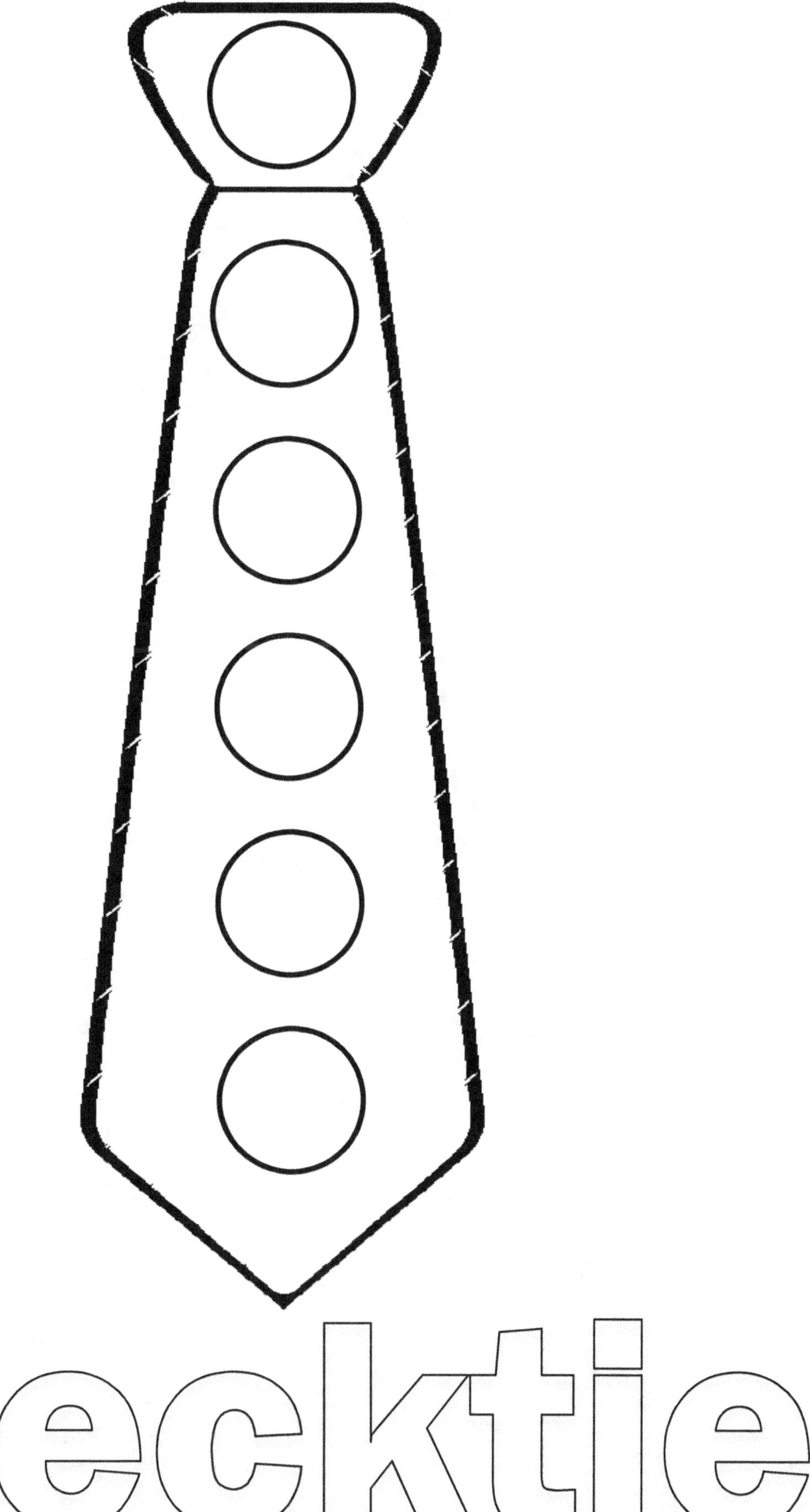

Necktie

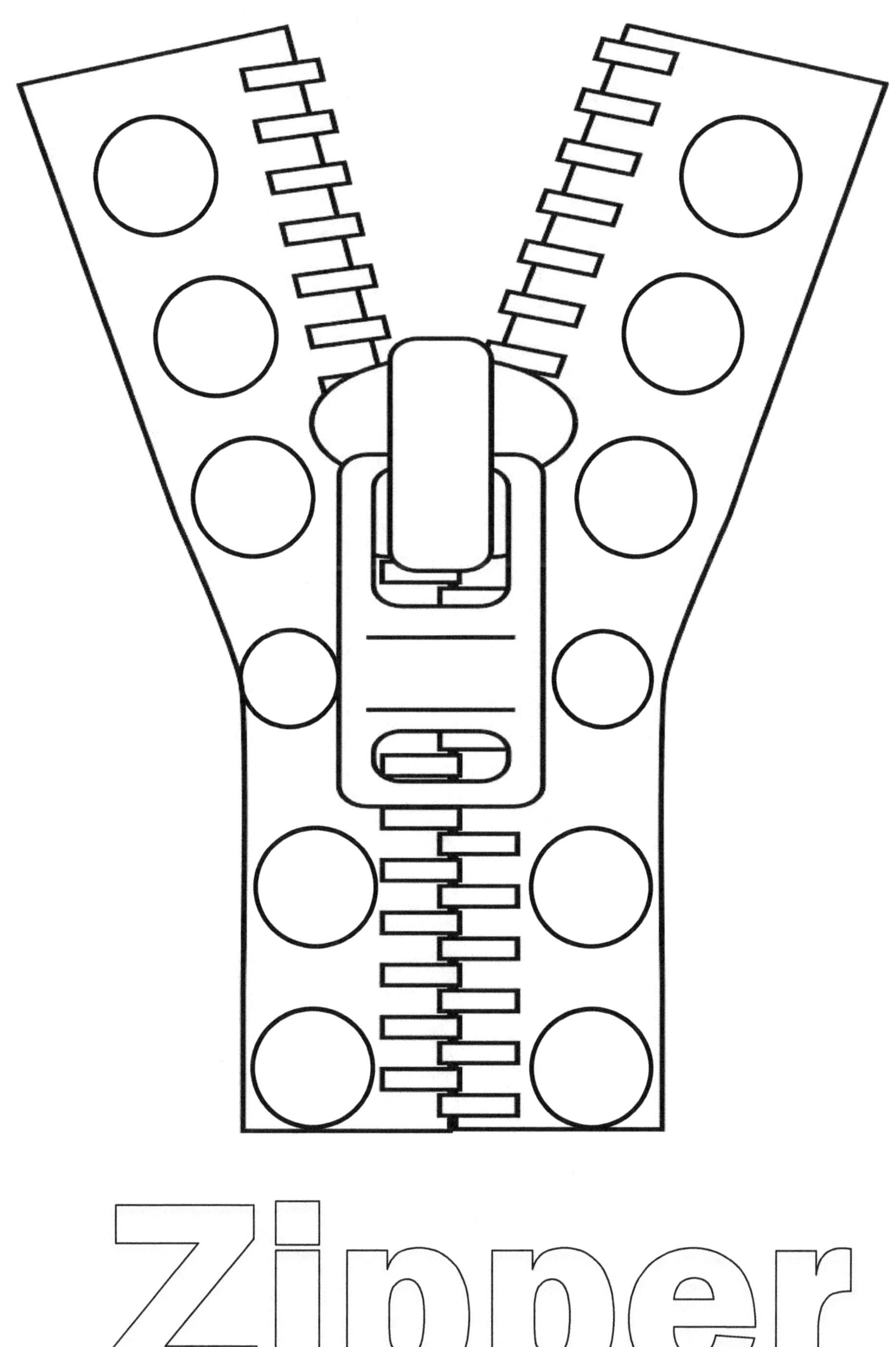

Zipper

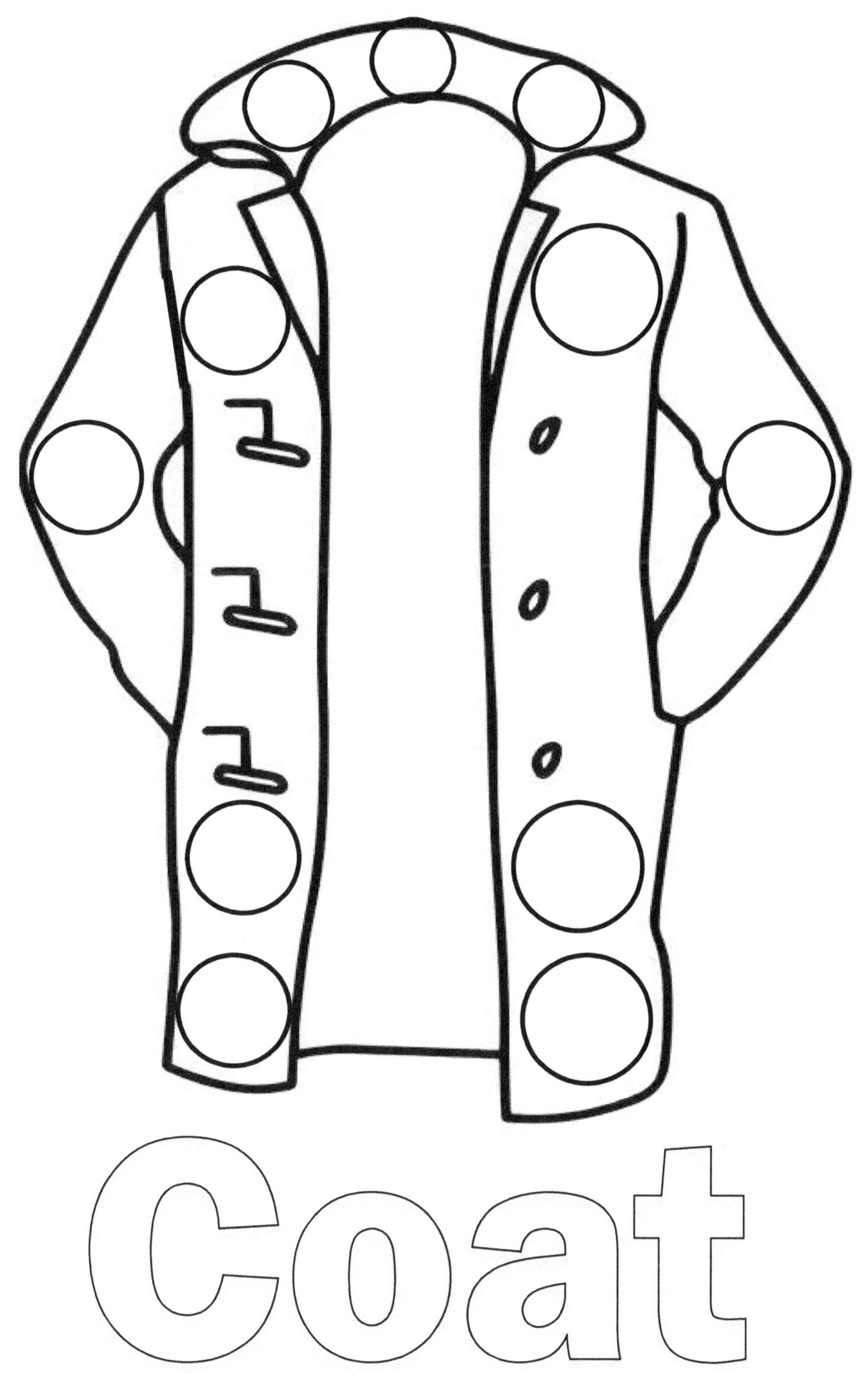

Coat

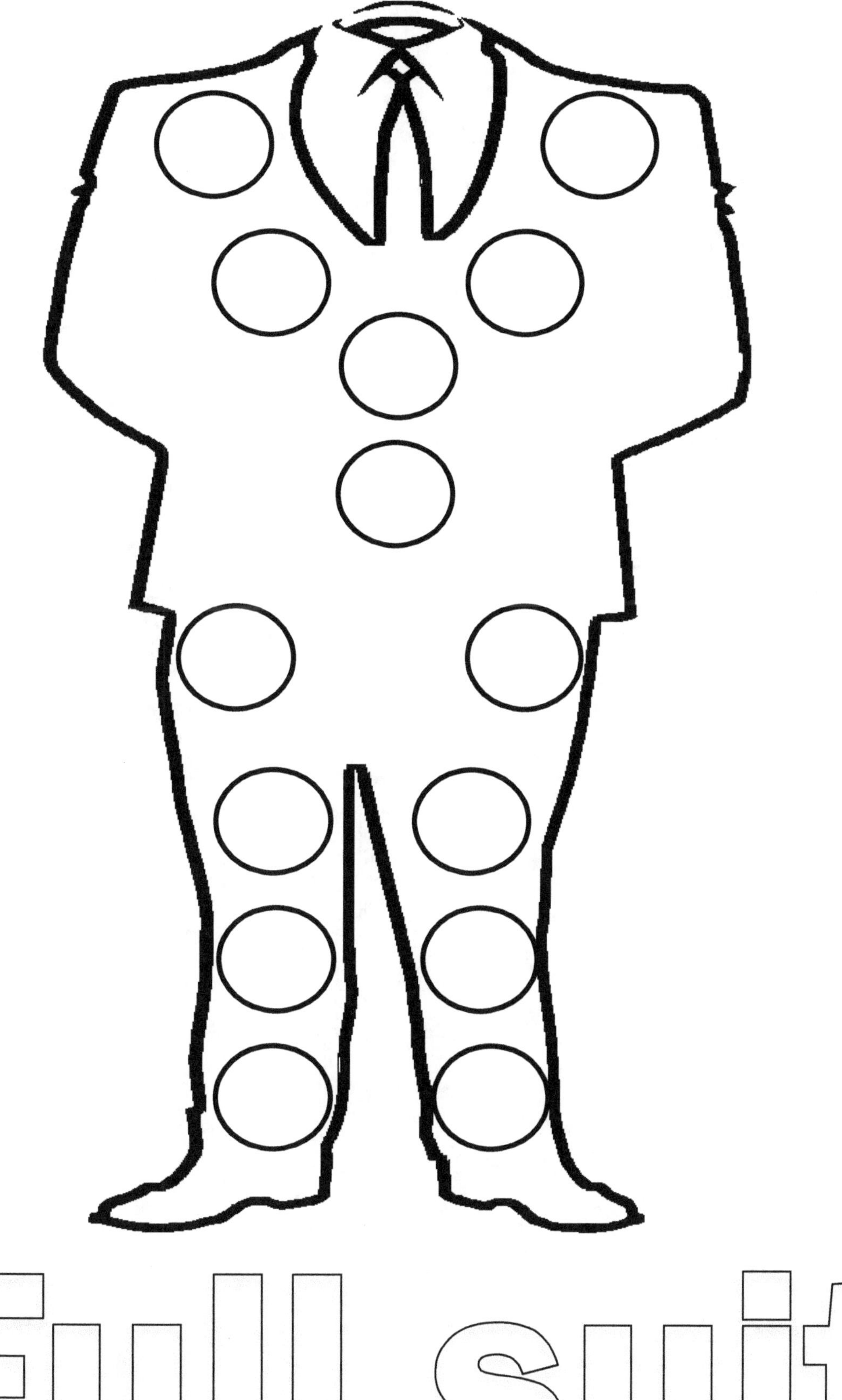

Full suit

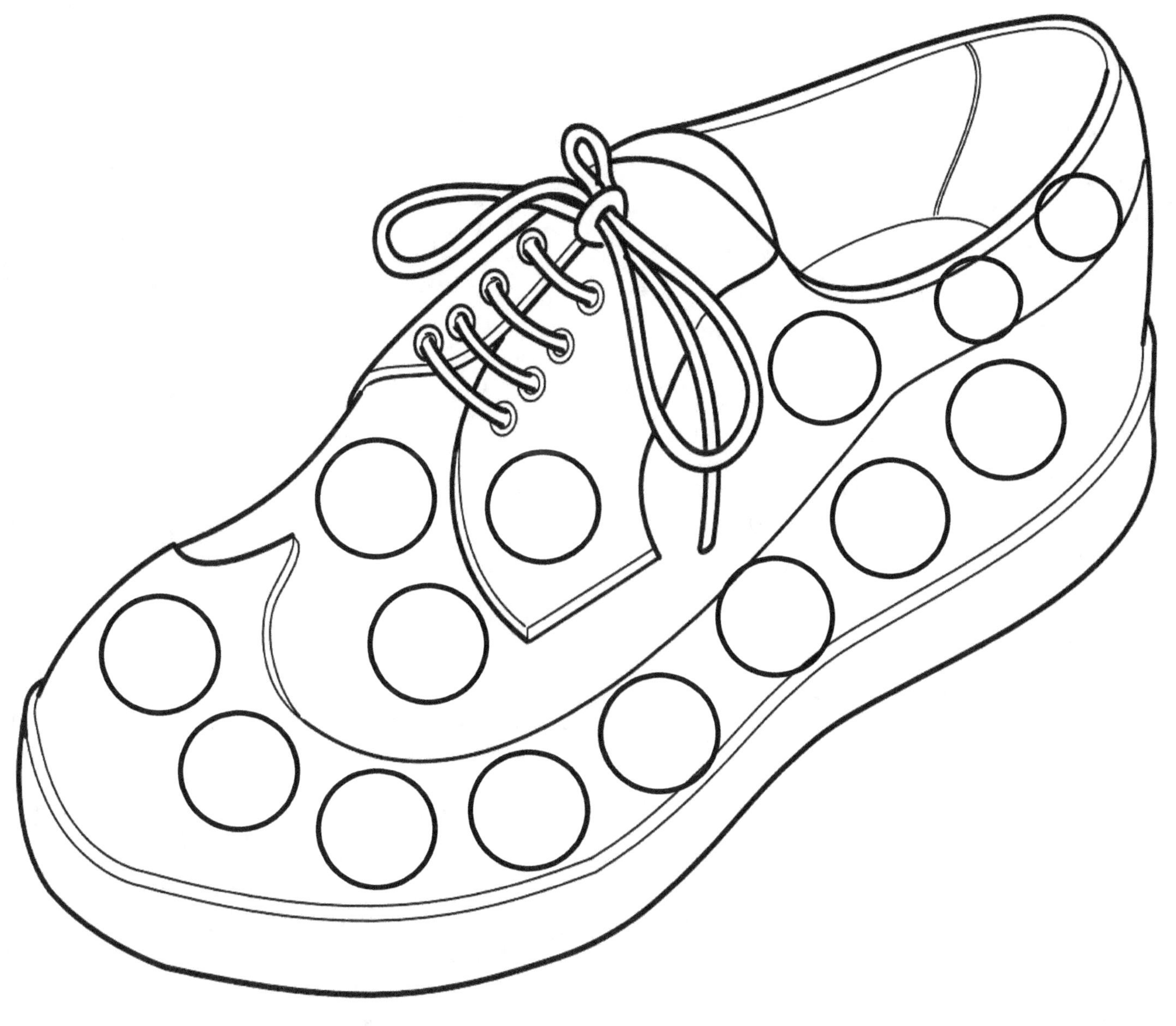

Shoe

Athletic shoe

High heel
shoe

Skating shoe

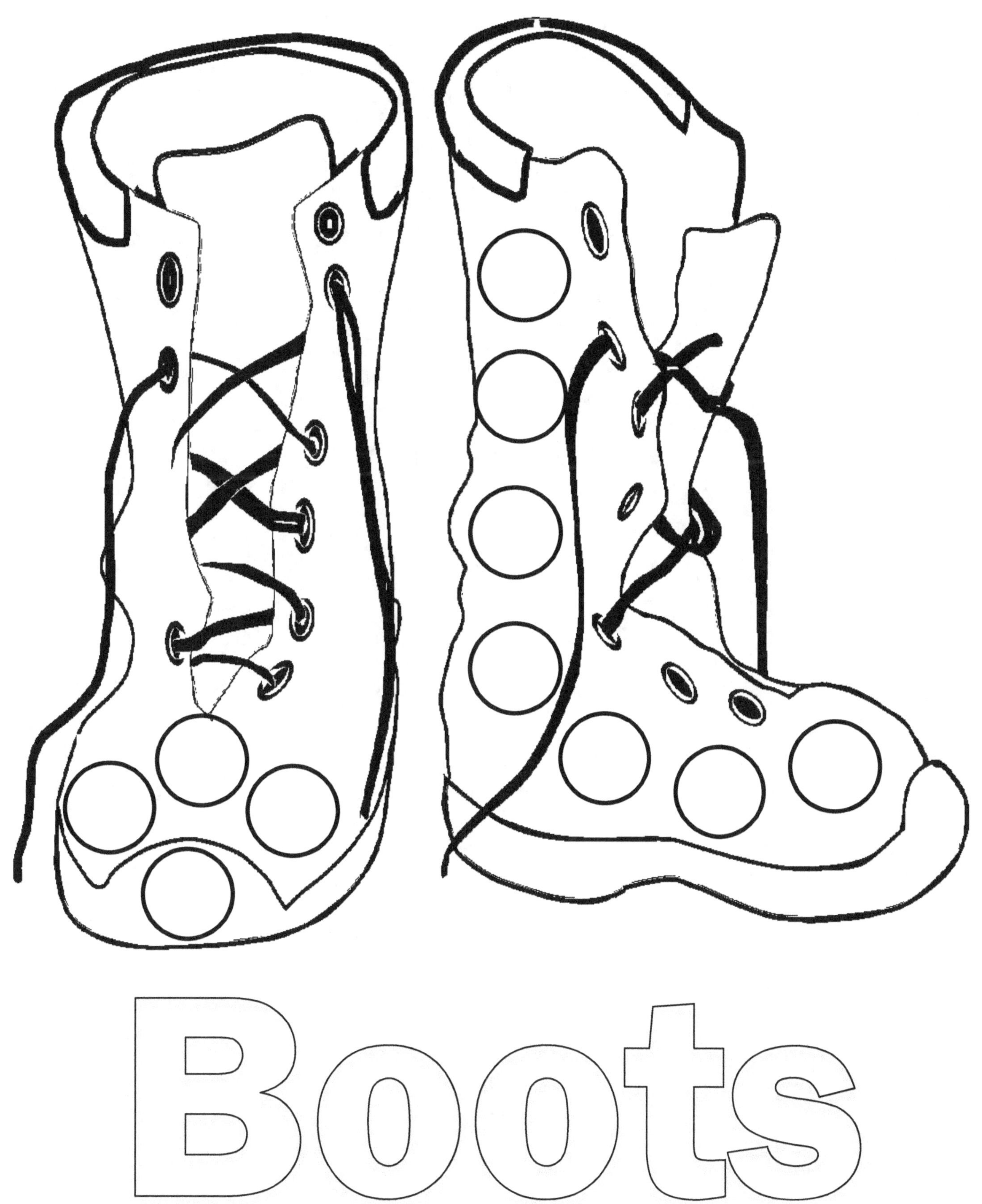
Boots

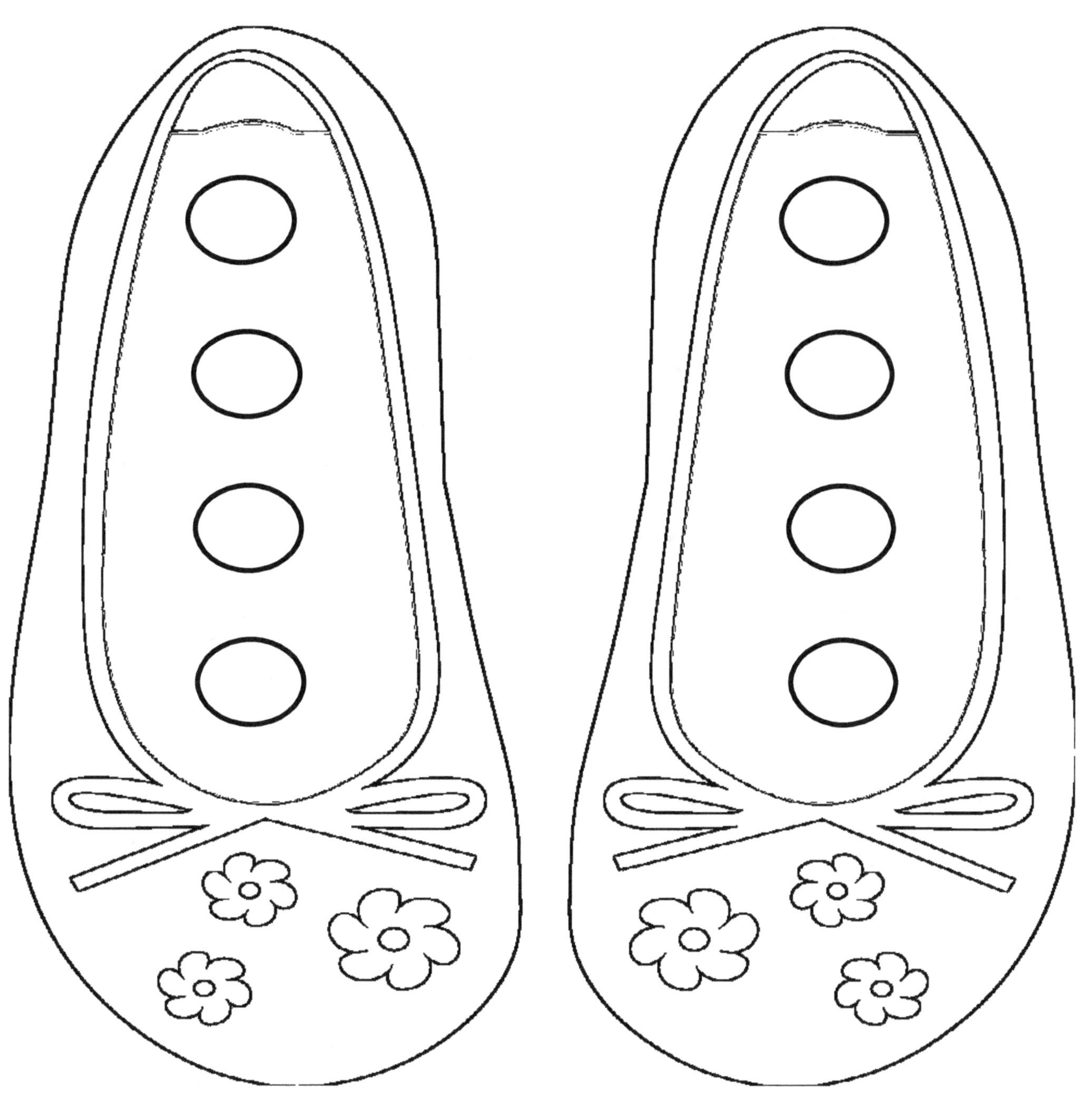

Women's shoes

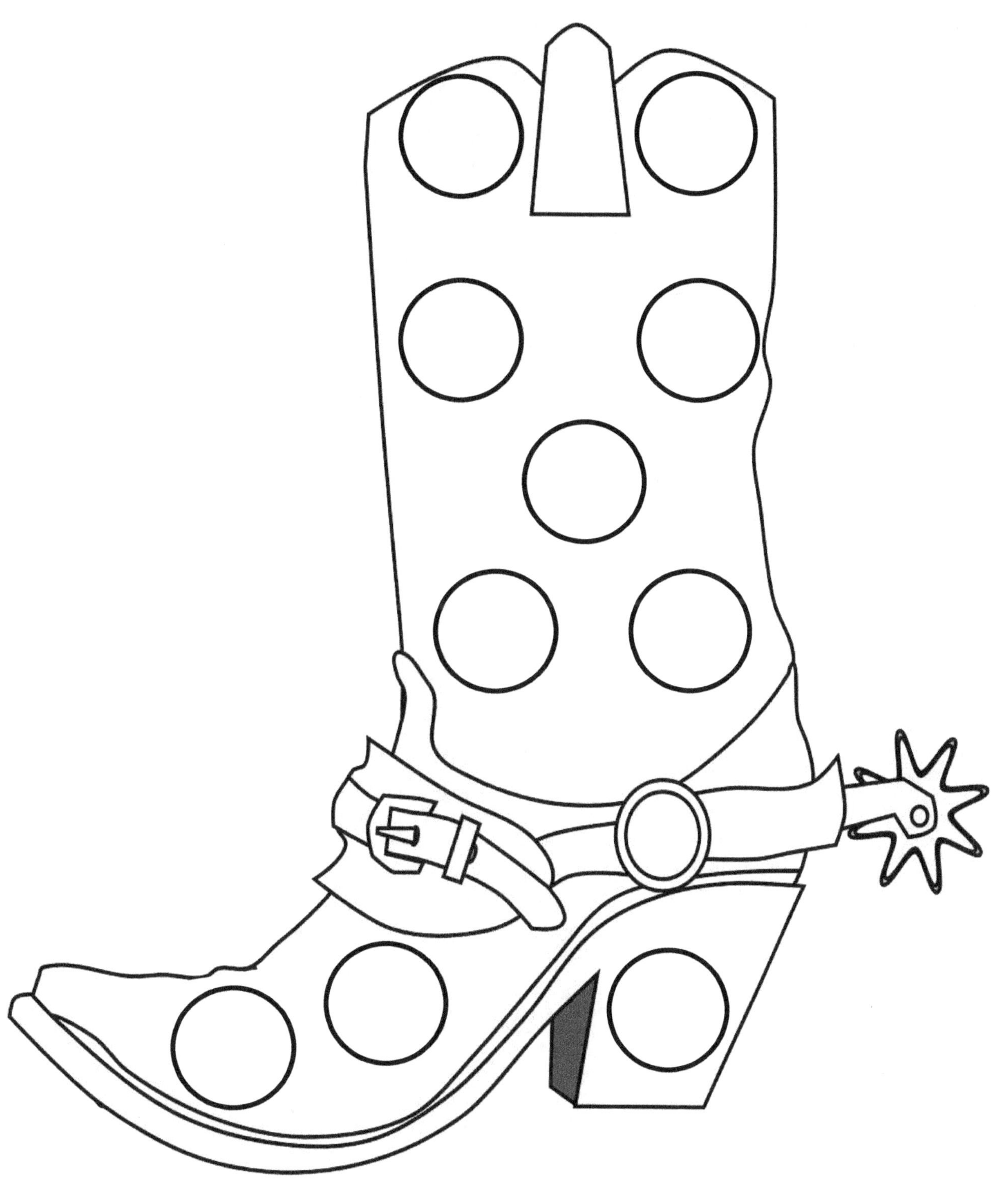

Cowboy boots

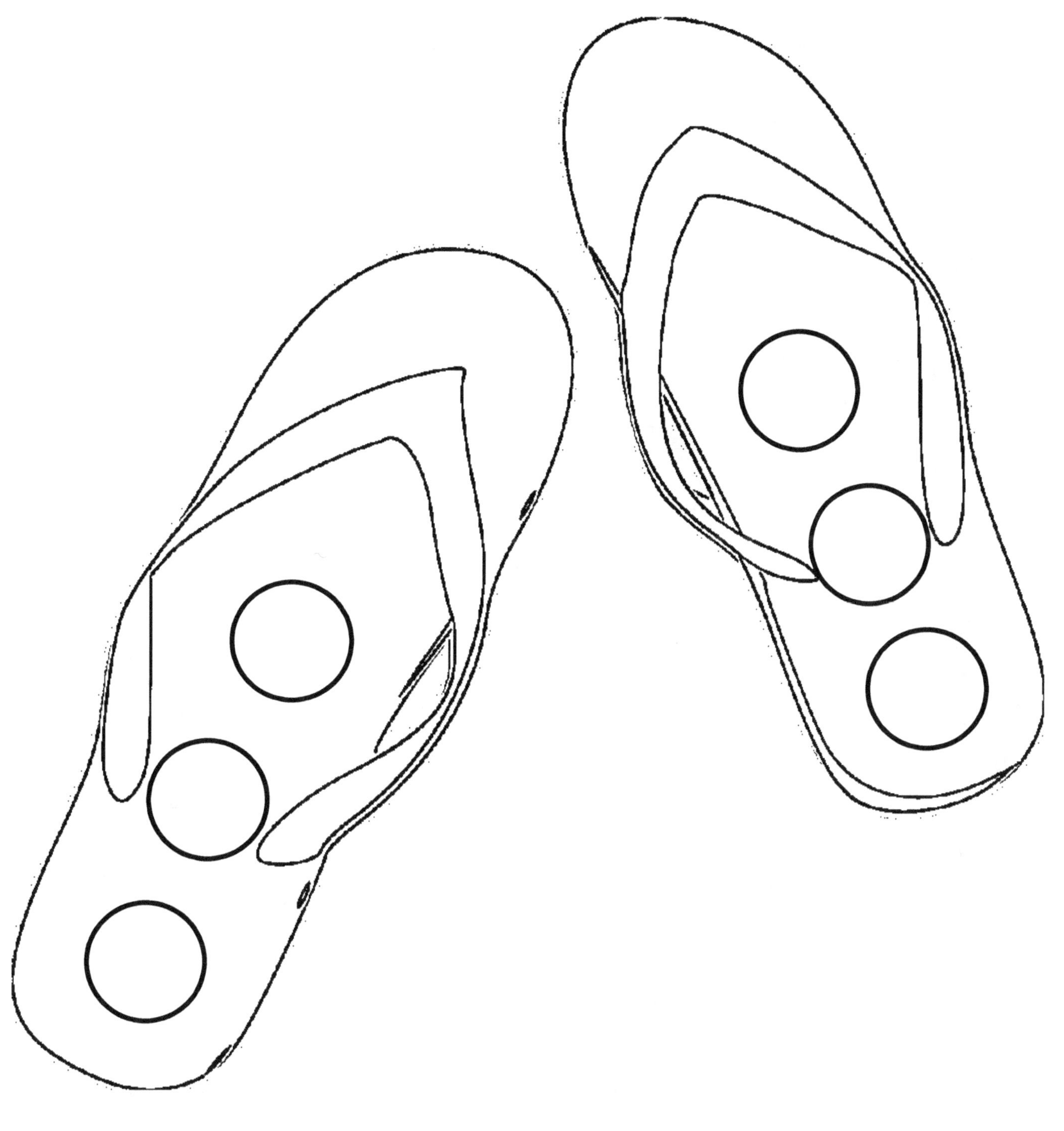

Flip flops

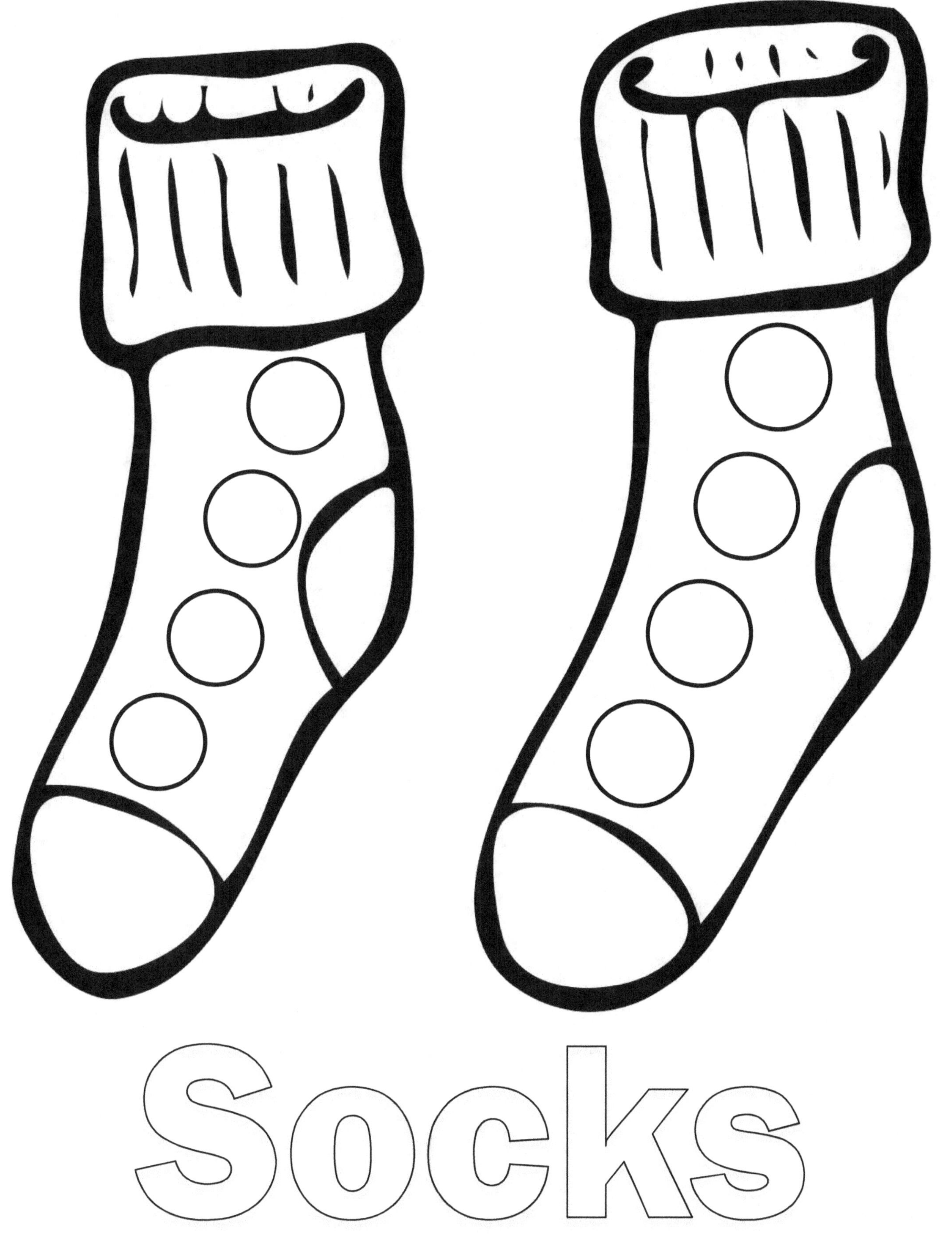
Socks

Dress

Wedding dress

Skirt

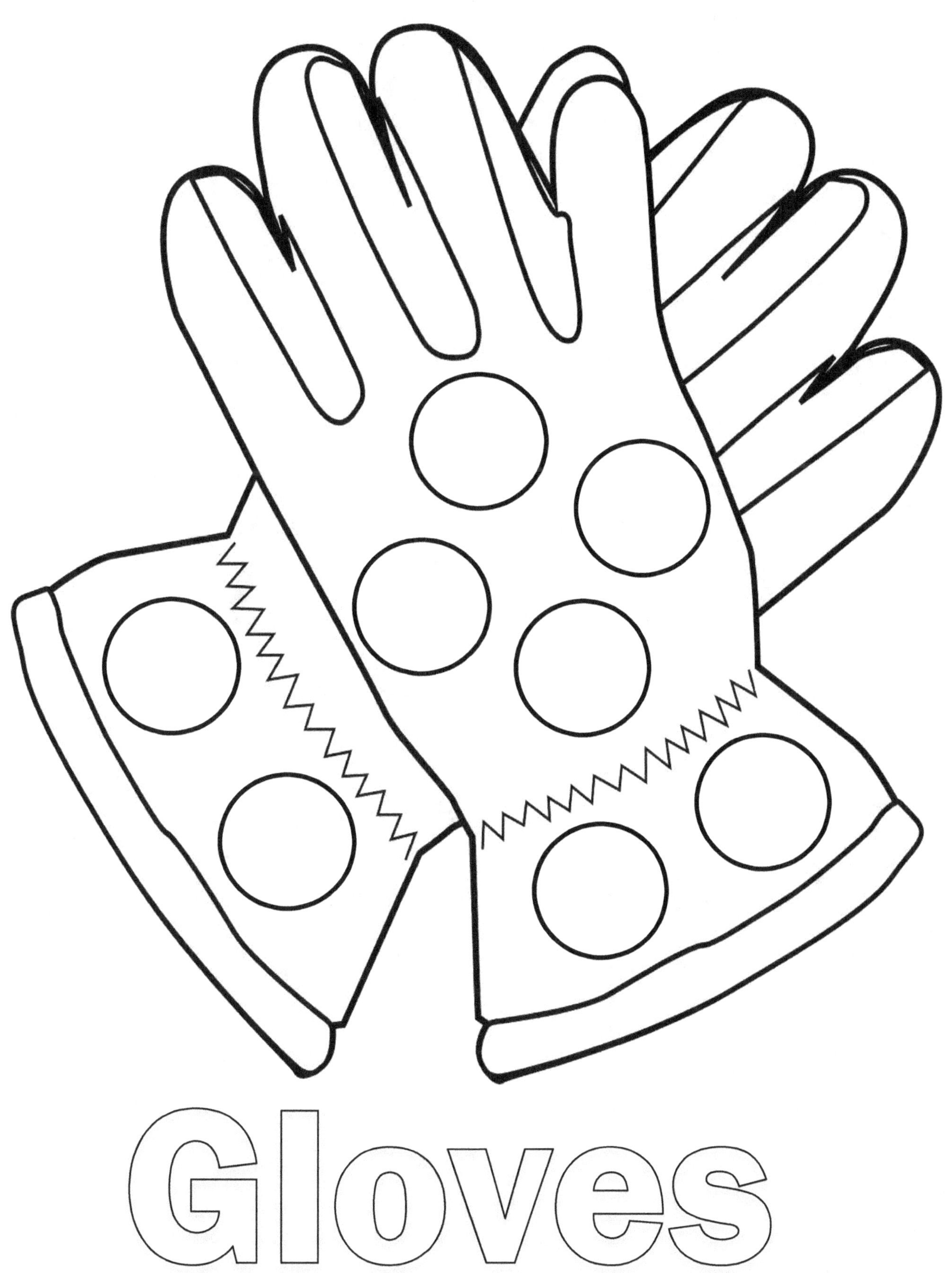

Gloves

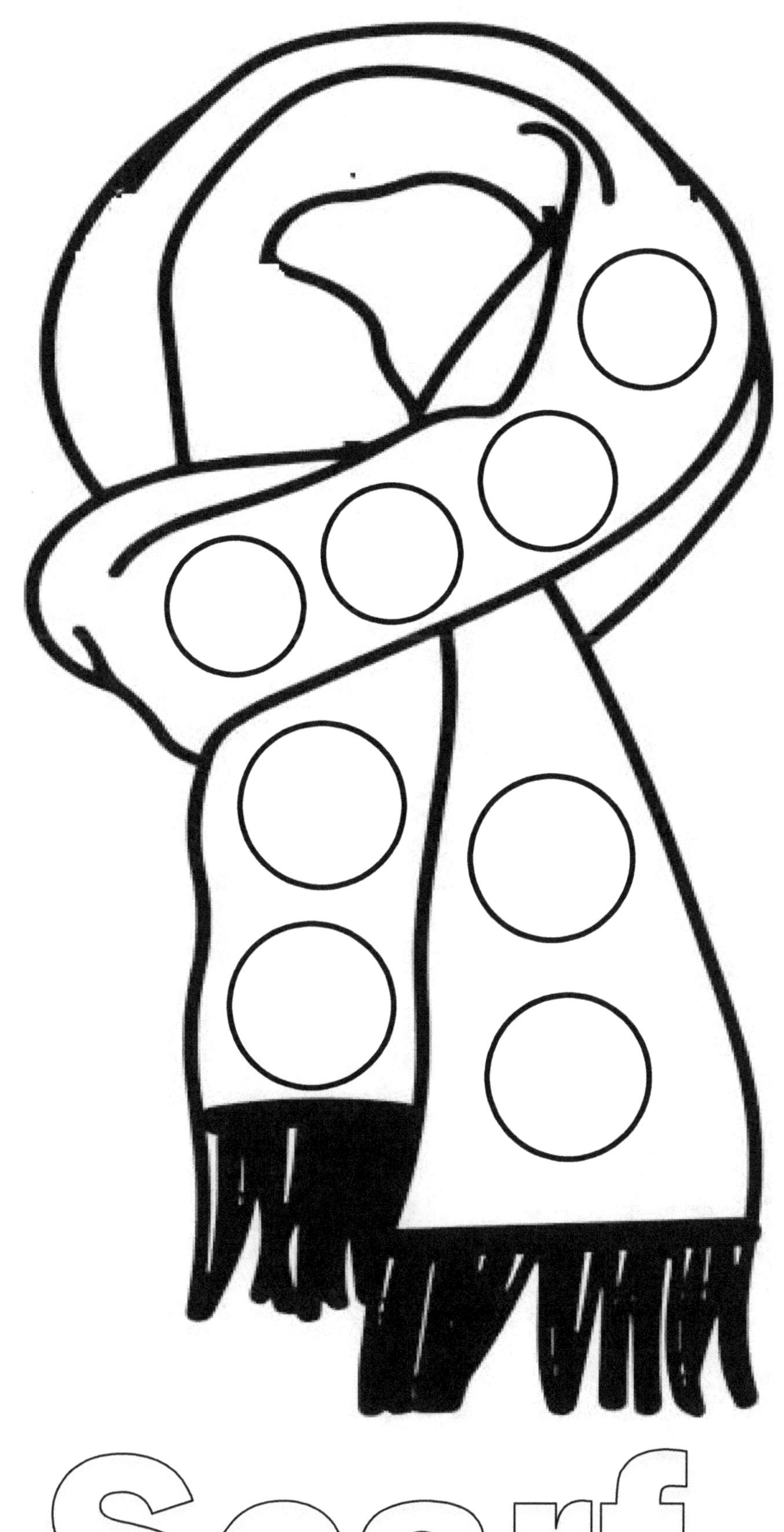

Scarf

wardrobe

Don't forget to put

your clothes in the

wardrobe

www.ingramcontent.com/pod-product-compliance
Lightning Source LLC
Chambersburg PA
CBHW082344270726
48658CB00017B/3119